SUPERSPORTS
INFOGRAPHICS

SUPER HOCKEY INFOGRAPHICS

Jeff Savage

graphics by
Vic Kulihin

Lerner Publications • Minneapolis

Lerner Publications Company
A division of Lerner Publishing Group, Inc.
241 First Avenue North
Minneapolis, MN 55401 USA

For reading levels and more information, look up this title at www.lernerbooks.com.

Main text set in Univers LT Std 12/15.
Typeface provided by Adobe Systems.

Library of Congress Cataloging-in-Publication Data

Savage, Jeff, 1961–
        Super hockey infographics / by Jeff Savage ; illustrated by Vic Kulihin.
            p.   cm. — (Super sports infographics)
        Includes index.
        ISBN 978-1-4677-5234-3 (lib. bdg. : alk. paper)
        ISBN 978-1-4677-7577-9 (pbk.)
        ISBN 978-1-4677-6278-6 (EB pdf)
        1. Hockey—Graphic methods—Juvenile literature.
    I. Kulihin, Vic, ill. II. Title.
    GV847.25.S27 2015
    796.962'021—dc23   2014012457

Manufactured in the United States of America
1 – DP – 12/31/14

CONTENTS

Introduction: Let's Play Hockey! • 4

A GROWING LEAGUE • 6

SCORING WITH AUDIENCES • 8

COUNT ME IN • 10

GOING GLOBAL • 12

THE INTERNATIONAL STAGE • 14

POSITIONED FOR SUCCESS • 16

SCORE! • 18

GREATEST OF ALL TIME • 20

THE PRICE TO PLAY • 22

THE PUCK STOPS HERE • 24

HOCKEY VALUES • 26

THE STANLEY CUP • 28

Index • 32
Further Information • 31
Glossary • 30

LET'S PLAY HOCKEY!

Can you keep up with one of the fastest games in the world? Take this quiz to see how big a hockey fan you are.

1. Do you know why Wayne Gretzky's nickname is the Great One?

2. Have you ever imagined yourself playing hockey for your country in the Olympics?

3. Can you name the most successful team in the history of the National Hockey League (NHL)?

4. Do you know where most NHL players were born?

> Did you answer yes to any of these questions?

IF SO, CONGRATULATIONS!

You are officially a true hockey fanatic. Hockey is an exciting game loved by fans around the world. People began playing the sport in Canada in the 1800s, but a lot has changed since then. From peewee leagues to the Olympics to the NHL, there's plenty to learn about the spectacular sport of hockey. Wondering how to make sense of it all? Charts, graphs, and other infographics can help. Read on to discover some of the fascinating facts and figures behind this dynamic sport.

A GROWING LEAGUE

Since the NHL's first year in 1917, teams in the league have gone through many changes. Teams have been founded, relocated, contracted, and renamed. For the 2013–2014 season, the result of all these changes was a league of 30 teams, spread out all around the United States and Canada. You can see the first NHL season for each of the league's current franchises in this timeline. Some of the teams started out in different cities than the ones they play in now.

Chicago Blackhawks
Detroit Red Wings
New York Rangers

Boston Bruins

Montreal Canadiens
Toronto Maple Leafs

1926–1927

1924–1925

1917–1918

Carolina Hurricanes
Colorado Avalanche
Edmonton Oilers
Arizona Coyotes

Winnipeg Jets

Ottawa Senators
Tampa Bay Lightning

2000–
2001

1999–
2000

1998–
1999

1993–
1994

1992–
1993

1991–
1992

Calgary Flames
New York Islanders

1979–
1980

1974–
1975

1972–
1973

1970–
1971

1967–
1968

San Jose Sharks

Anaheim Ducks
Florida Panthers

Buffalo Sabres
Vancouver Canucks

Nashville Predators

Dallas Stars
Los Angeles Kings
Philadelphia Flyers
Pittsburgh Penguins
St. Louis Blues

New Jersey Devils
Washington Capitals

Columbus Blue Jackets
Minnesota Wild

SCORING WITH AUDIENCES

Hockey is on the rise in the United States. In a 2012 survey by the Harris Poll asking people to pick their favorite sport to follow, hockey came in at number six. That may not sound terribly impressive (and it's true that hockey took just 5 percent of the vote), but when you take a closer look, you'll see that hockey is more popular now than ever before.

In 1985, the first year the Harris Poll was taken, hockey got just 2 percent of the vote. It tied for 12th place. Since then, its number of fans has climbed steadily. In fact, these days, hockey is 150 percent more popular than it was in 1985! What's more, it has surged past five other sports. Check out the graph to the right to see just how popular hockey is compared to other sports—and how its popularity has grown over time. (The percentages may not add up to 100 percent because the numbers have been rounded.)

hockey
auto racing
baseball
bowling
college football
horse racing
men's college basketball
men's golf
men's pro basketball
men's soccer
men's tennis
pro football
track and field

1985   1990

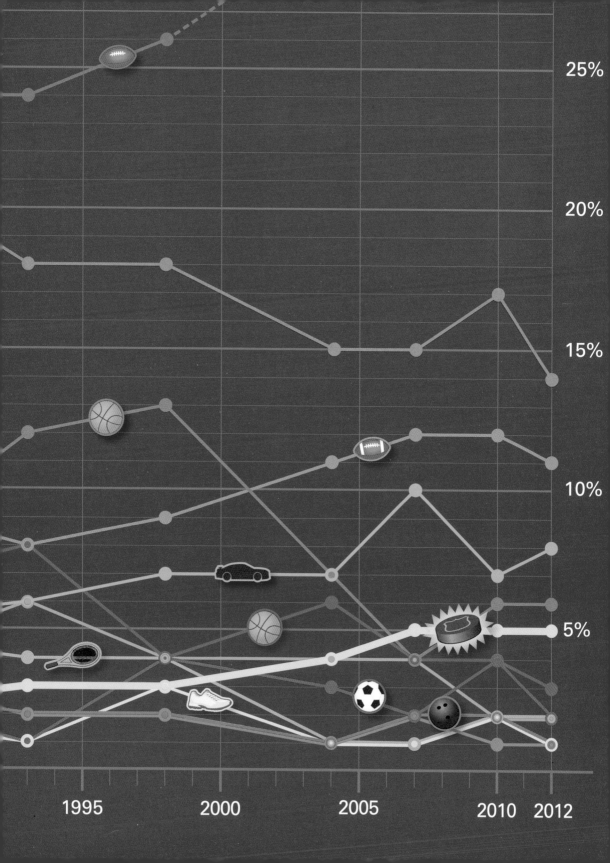

25%

20%

15%

10%

5%

1995   2000   2005   2010   2012

COUNT ME IN

More people are playing hockey than ever before. USA Hockey is the official governing organization for the sport in the United States. It keeps statistics about how many people hit the ice each year. Since the 1990–1991 season, when those statistics were first shared with the public, participation in hockey has skyrocketed. You can see in these graphics how the sport has grown, and the six states where participation grew the most between the 2010–2011 and 2011–2012 seasons. The numbers on the pucks represent the number of people playing hockey in the United States that season.

439,140

421,399

384,779

350,007

262,873

195,125

| 1990–1991 | 1992–1993 | 1994–1995 | 1996–1997 | 1998–1999 | 2000–2001 |

These are the six states where hockey participation grew the most between the 2010–2011 and 2011–2012 seasons:

Hawaii 71.4%
Mississippi 55.9%
Iowa 16%
Virginia 13.9%
Oregon 13.4%
Arizona 12.7%

446,328 — 2002–2003
445,245 — 2004–2005
457,038 — 2006–2007
465,975 — 2008–2009
500,579 — 2010–2011
510,279 — 2012–2013

GOING GLOBAL

In the NHL's long history, players from 30 countries around the world have competed in the league. In 2013–2014, 17 countries were represented. It's no surprise that Canada leads the way, with more than half of all NHL players in 2014 originating in that nation. Take a look at the countries of origin for all current players in the NHL as of May 2014.

Canada
510
(51.8%)

United States
242 (24.6%)

Czech Republic
37 (3.8%)

France
2 (0.2%)

Switzerland
11 (1.1%)

Austria
3 (0.3%)

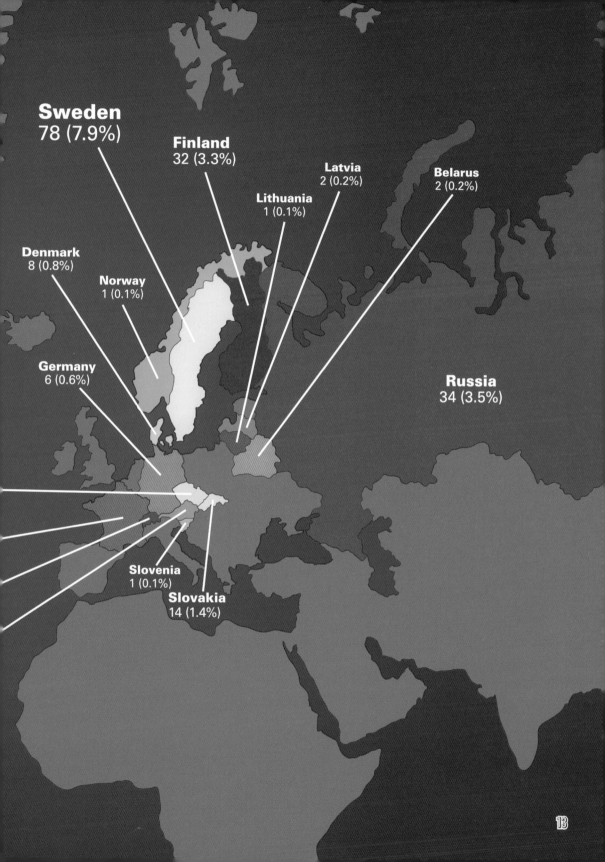

Sweden
78 (7.9%)

Finland
32 (3.3%)

Latvia
2 (0.2%)

Belarus
2 (0.2%)

Lithuania
1 (0.1%)

Denmark
8 (0.8%)

Norway
1 (0.1%)

Germany
6 (0.6%)

Russia
34 (3.5%)

Slovenia
1 (0.1%)

Slovakia
14 (1.4%)

THE INTERNATIONAL STAGE

Men's ice hockey became an official Olympic sport at the 1920 Winter Olympic Games in Antwerp, Belgium. But it would be 78 years before the International Olympic Committee (IOC) added women's hockey to the Winter Games. Check out all the men's and women's teams that have taken home the top Olympic hockey prize and when they did it.

OLYMPIC GOLD MEDAL-WINNING HOCKEY TEAMS

Canada

VII OLYMPICS — 1920
I OLYMPICS — 1924
OLYMPICS — 1928
OLYMPICS — 1932
V OLYMPICS — 1948
VII OLYMPICS — 1952
XIX OLYMPICS — 2002
OLYMPICS — 2010
OLYMPICS — 2014

XIX OLYMPICS — 2002
XX OLYMPICS — 2006
OLYMPICS — 2010
OLYMPICS — 2014

POSITIONED FOR SUCCESS

NHL rules state that teams must have 20 players dressed and ready to play for each game. Hockey teams are made up of centers, wings, defenders, and goalies. It's up to coaches to decide how many players at each position to dress for games. The graphics below show how most NHL coaches fill out their rosters. You can also see where each position generally plays on the ice.

The **goalie** has only one job: keep the puck out of the net.

The main job of **defenders** is to keep the other team from scoring.

The **center** takes faceoffs and is usually the leader on the ice.

Wings battle for the puck along the boards.

HERE'S HOW MOST NHL COACHES FILL OUT THEIR ROSTERS FOR GAMES:

Goalies
2

Centers
4

Wings
8

Defenders
6

Defenders are often the biggest players on a hockey team.

Wings are called left wings or right wings depending on which side of the rink they play.

SCORE!

People love to have debates about famous athletes. Arguing about the greatest quarterback or home run hitter in history is a favorite pastime of sports fans. But there is no debate about the top offensive player in NHL history. Wayne Gretzky (1978–1999) scored, by far, more combined goals and assists than anyone else. He did this despite playing in nearly 300 fewer games than the three players who came closest to his record. That's why Gretzky's nickname is simply the Great One. If you're still in doubt, check out the stats. Here are the 13 highest-scoring players in NHL history as of the end of the 2013–2014 season.

Gordie Howe
- 801
- 1,049
- 1,850
- 1,767

Mark Messier
- 694
- 1,193
- 1,887
- 1,756

- ○ Goals
- ○ Assists
- ● Total points
- ◌ Games played

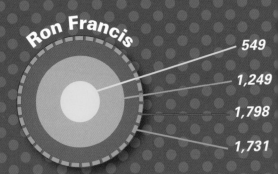

Ron Francis
- 549
- 1,249
- 1,798
- 1,731

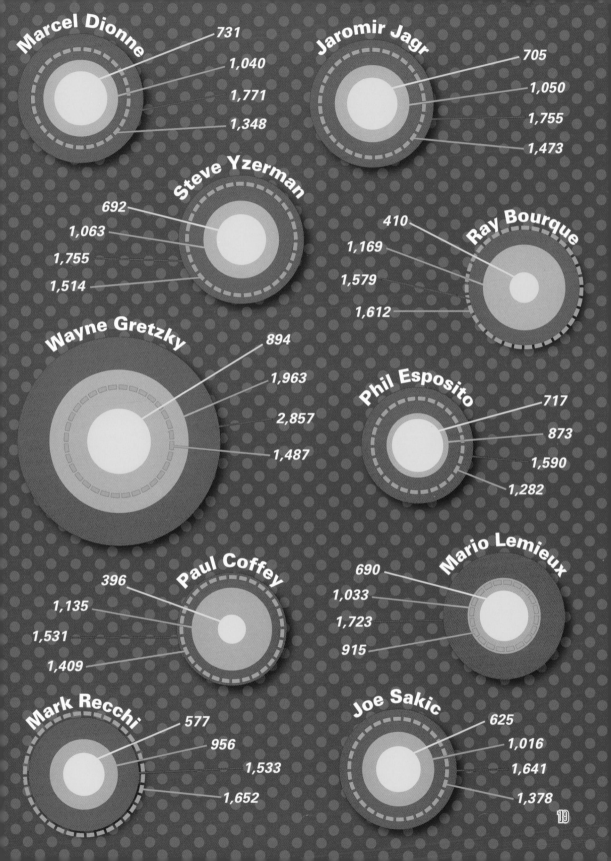

Marcel Dionne
731
1,040
1,771
1,348

Jaromir Jagr
705
1,050
1,755
1,473

Steve Yzerman
692
1,063
1,755
1,514

Ray Bourque
410
1,169
1,579
1,612

Wayne Gretzky
894
1,963
2,857
1,487

Phil Esposito
717
873
1,590
1,282

Paul Coffey
396
1,135
1,531
1,409

Mario Lemieux
690
1,033
1,723
915

Mark Recchi
577
956
1,533
1,652

Joe Sakic
625
1,016
1,641
1,378

GREATEST OF ALL TIME

You know that Wayne Gretzky is the greatest NHL player ever in goals and assists scored. But do you know how he compares to players in other sports? Like the NHL, the National Basketball Association (NBA), the National Football League (NFL), and Major League Baseball (MLB) all give out Most Valuable Player (MVP) awards each season. Take a look at how many MVP awards each sport's standout athletes have snagged. Each puck or ball represents one MVP award.

HOCKEY

GRETZKY

HOWE

SHORE

LEMIEUX

OVECHKIN

CLARKE

ORR

MORENZ

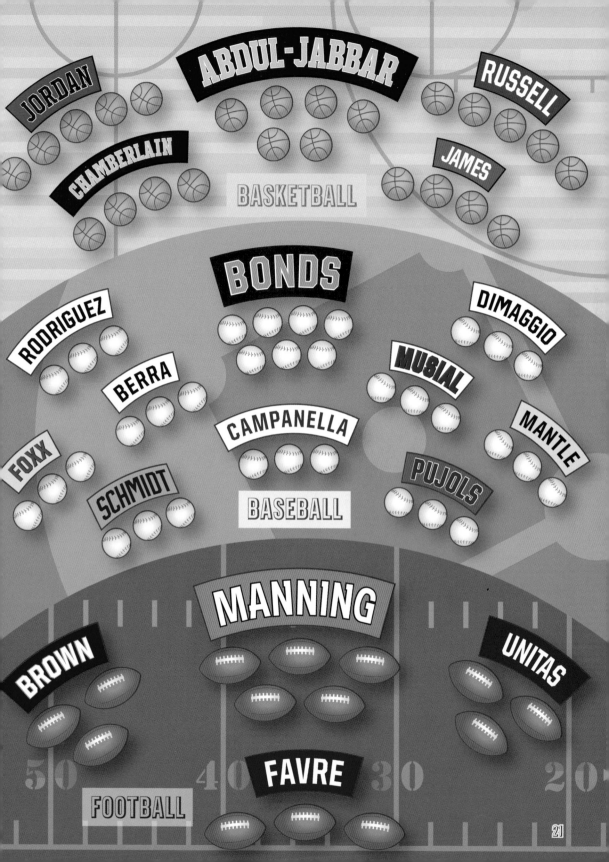

JORDAN

ABDUL-JABBAR

RUSSELL

CHAMBERLAIN

JAMES

BASKETBALL

BONDS

RODRIGUEZ

DIMAGGIO

BERRA

MUSIAL

FOXX

CAMPANELLA

MANTLE

SCHMIDT

PUJOLS

BASEBALL

MANNING

BROWN

UNITAS

50   40   FAVRE   30   20

FOOTBALL

21

THE PRICE TO PLAY

Do you want to be the next great one? Maybe you can picture yourself helping win a hockey gold medal for your country. First, you need to gear up. But get ready to pay up as well! The equipment worn by hockey players is expensive. Here's how much money standard hockey equipment costs compared to what is needed for some other sports. These are average costs from 2013 for equipment for young people in the United States and Canada, so you might find different prices at your local sporting goods store.

HOCKEY

helmet $105

jersey $90

pads for elbows, shoulders, knees, thighs, and more $175

gloves $64

stick $46

skates $200

puck $3

THE PUCK STOPS HERE

If a hard rubber disk speeds toward you at 100 miles (161 kilometers) per hour, you should duck! But goaltenders can't get out of the way. They have to stand there and take it. With a glove on one hand and a stick in the other, goalies are the last line of defense on a hockey rink.

In the NHL, the goal is 6 feet (1.8 meters) wide and 4 feet (1.2 m) high. Protecting the net requires concentration and cat-quick reflexes. Take a look at the goalies who have the most wins and shutouts in NHL history through the end of the 2013–2014 season.

MOST SHUTOUTS BY GOALIES

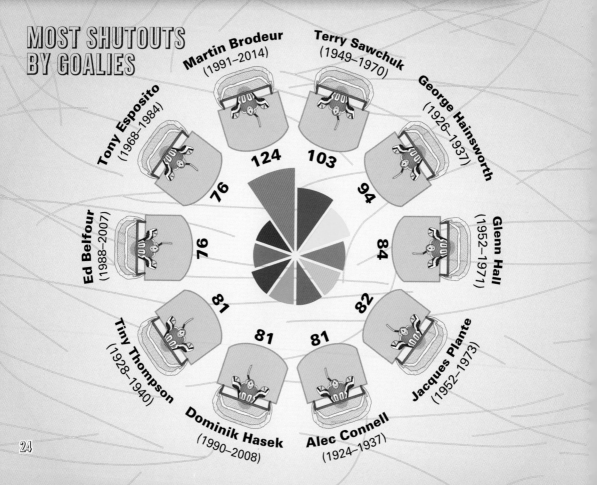

Martin Brodeur (1991–2014) — 124

Terry Sawchuk (1949–1970) — 103

George Hainsworth (1926–1937) — 94

Glenn Hall (1952–1971) — 84

Jacques Plante (1952–1973) — 82

Alec Connell (1924–1937) — 81

Dominik Hasek (1990–2008) — 81

Tiny Thompson (1928–1940) — 81

Ed Belfour (1988–2007) — 76

Tony Esposito (1968–1984) — 76

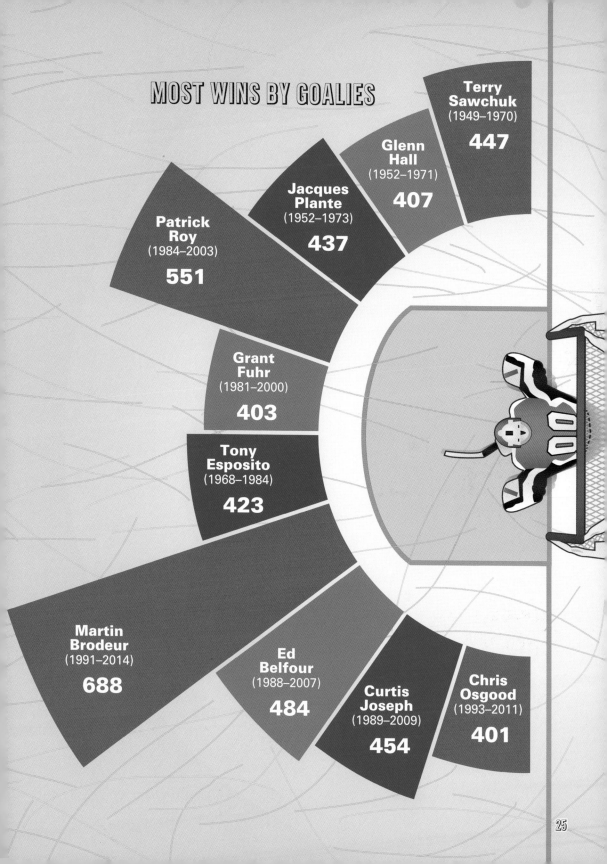

MOST WINS BY GOALIES

Terry Sawchuk (1949–1970) **447**

Glenn Hall (1952–1971) **407**

Jacques Plante (1952–1973) **437**

Patrick Roy (1984–2003) **551**

Grant Fuhr (1981–2000) **403**

Tony Esposito (1968–1984) **423**

Martin Brodeur (1991–2014) **688**

Ed Belfour (1988–2007) **484**

Curtis Joseph (1989–2009) **454**

Chris Osgood (1993–2011) **401**

HOCKEY VALUES

How much money would you pay to buy an NHL team? If you took up a collection from everyone you knew, you'd probably still need to borrow more—a lot more. The map on the right shows how much each of the 10 most valuable NHL franchises was worth in 2013, according to *Forbes* magazine.

Vancouver Canucks
$700 million

Los Angeles Kings
$450 million

TOP 10 HIGHEST AVERAGES FOR A SINGLE TICKET IN 2013–2014

Pittsburgh Penguins	$204
Boston Bruins	$223
New York Rangers	$233
Montreal Canadiens	$257
Calgary Flames	$262
Vancouver Canucks	$265
Edmonton Oilers	$273
Winnipeg Jets	$277
Chicago Blackhawks	$313
Toronto Maple Leafs	$369

Toronto
Maple Leafs
$1.15 billion

Montreal
Canadiens
$775 million

Boston Bruins
$600 million

Detroit
Red Wings
$470 million

Chicago
Blackhawks
$625 million

Pittsburgh
Penguins
$480 million

New York
Rangers
$850 million

Philadelphia
Flyers
$500 million

THE STANLEY CUP

A trophy symbolizes greatness. The Wimbledon Gentlemen's Singles trophy (tennis), the Vince Lombardi Trophy (NFL), and the Heisman Trophy (college football) are all well-known symbols of excellence. But perhaps the most famous sports trophy is the NHL's Stanley Cup. It is named for Frederick Arthur Stanley, who donated the trophy in 1892 to be awarded to the "championship hockey club" of Canada. Since 1926, the Stanley Cup has been presented to the NHL's top team. These are the 12 teams that have hoisted the Stanley Cup most often in the NHL since 1926.

22

Montreal Canadiens

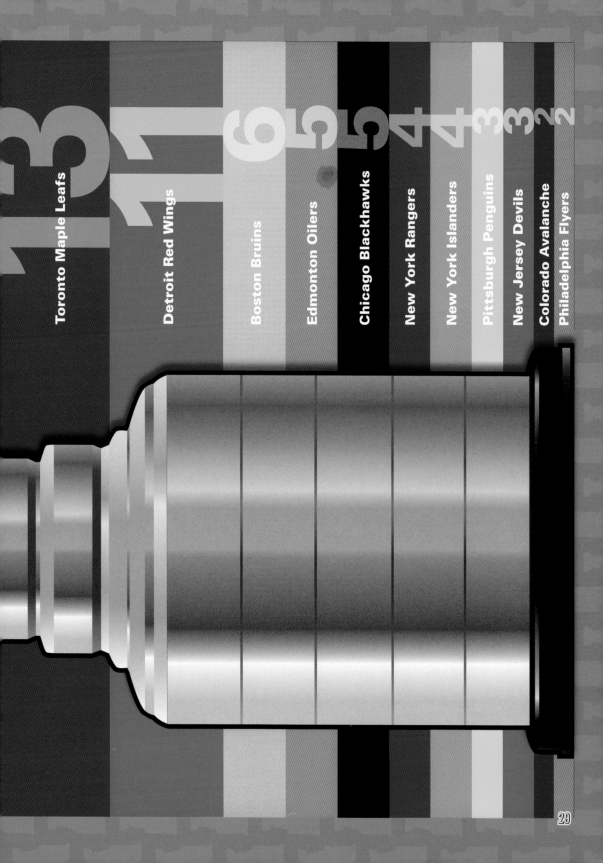

13 Toronto Maple Leafs

11 Detroit Red Wings

6 Boston Bruins

5 Edmonton Oilers

5 Chicago Blackhawks

4 New York Rangers

4 New York Islanders

3 Pittsburgh Penguins

3 New Jersey Devils

2 Colorado Avalanche

2 Philadelphia Flyers

Glossary

ASSIST: an assist is awarded to up to two players who helped their team score a goal

CENTER: the player who skates in the center of the ice. Each team usually has one center on the ice at a time.

DEFENDER: a player whose main job is to stop the opponent from scoring. Two of each team's six players on the ice are usually defenders.

FOUND: to set up or establish

FRANCHISE: a sports team's entire organization, including players, coaches, office staff, and more

ORGANIZATION: a group of people who work together for a purpose

POLL: a study in which questions are asked and answers are received in order to learn results

RELOCATE: to move a team to a new city

SHUTOUT: a game in which the opposing team doesn't score any points

SOVIET UNION: Russia and other republics in Europe and Asia that broke apart in 1991

STATISTICS: information, often in the form of numbers, used to determine the value or meaning of something

UNIFIED TEAM: a group of some former republics of the Soviet Union that competed at the Olympic Games

WING: a player who skates near the side boards. Each team usually has two wings on the ice at a time.

Further Information

Hockey News
http://www.thehockeynews.com
This popular site provides fans with the latest news and rumors about hockey from the NHL to the Olympics and much more.

Kennedy, Mike, and Mark Stewart. *Score!: The Action and Artistry of Hockey's Magnificent Moment.* Spectacular Sports series. Minneapolis: Millbrook Press, 2011. This book covers all aspects of scoring in the fastest game on ice.

Official NHL Site
http://www.nhl.com
The official National Hockey League website provides fans with the latest news about the league, biographies of players and coaches, and videos of game action.

Savage, Jeff. *Alex Ovechkin.* Amazing Athletes series. Minneapolis: Lerner Publications, 2012. This book takes you through the life of one of hockey's great current stars.

Sports Illustrated Kids
http://www.sikids.com
The *Sports Illustrated Kids* website provides information on all sports, including hockey.

Sports Illustrated Kids Stats!: The Greatest Numbers in Sports. New York: Sports Illustrated Kids, 2013. This book has lots of amazing statistics for all sports.

USA Hockey
http://www.usahockey.com
The official site of USA Hockey provides the latest news on youth teams and offers information and advice for parents and youth on playing hockey.

Yahoo Sports
http://sports.yahoo.com/blogs/nhl -puck-daddy
This well-written blog features offbeat stories and impressions of the current action in the NHL.

Index

goalie records, 24–25
Gretzky, Wayne "the Great One," 4, 18–20

hockey equipment costs, 22–23
hockey participation, 10–11
hockey popularity, 8–9
hockey positions, 16–17

MVP awards, 20–21

NHL franchises, 6–7

NHL franchise values, 26–27
NHL highest-scoring players, 18–19
NHL player nationalities, 12–13

Olympic gold-medal winning hockey teams, 14–15

Stanley, Frederick Arthur, 28
Stanley Cup winners, 28–29

USA Hockey, 10